MUST TRY HARDER!

Science

Constable & Robinson Ltd
55-56 Russell Square
London WC1B 4HP

www.constablerobinson.com

First published in the UK in 2013 by Constable,
an imprint of Constable & Robinson Ltd

Text © Constable & Robinson 2013
Compiled by Mark Leigh, Rod Green, Diane Law and Mike Haskins
Additional illustrations © 2013 Leah Barker

A copy of the British Library Cataloguing in Publication Data is
available from the British Library

ISBN 978-1-47211-385-6

Printed and bound by CPI Group (UK) Ltd, Croydon, CR0 4YY

10 9 8 7 6 5 4 3 2 1

MUST TRY HARDER!

Science

A. N. Teacher

INTRODUCTION

Your schooldays, however fondly you may remember them, are a minefield of potential classroom gaffes for students who are particularly naïve or who don't keep their wits about them. If it's true that we learn by making mistakes, then there are some poor pupils who must surely have been approaching genius level by the time they finally left the school gates behind forever, and it would seem that this has been the case ever since teachers first started chalking questions on a blackboard. Exam and homework blunders have provided endless amusement over the years with many appearing in print, the 19th century "Bulls and Blunders" being one early example. Such anthologies were especially popular in the 1930s, with Cecil Hunt's *Howlers* and Alexander Abingdon's *Boners* collections (illustrated by Dr Seuss) selling around the world, and inspiring many imitations.

The origins of these collections were complex. Clearly school teachers have always encountered weird and wacky mistakes on a daily basis – but sometimes they also turned these into teaching tools (what better way to bang home the right answer than to start with an example of a catastrophic mistake!) or adapted them for humorous purposes.

Today, our teachers continue to collect and share the most bizarre answers they find. Part of the joy of reading these comes from wondering what really happened. Is this a pupil desperately grasping for a half-remembered fact, or a surreal example of startling ignorance? Or is the student giving a knowingly cheeky, absurd answer, which might or might not amuse the teacher?

Either way, these blunders provide an ongoing source of fun. Here is the latest set of dispatches from the chalkface, in this case from the realm of Science, a discipline which is dedicated to clarifying and explaining the world around us, often to no avail . . .

SCIENCE

Name one way you can reduce your carbon footprint.

Wear smaller shoes

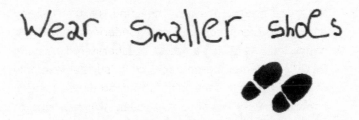

What significant invention enabled astronomers to understand that the earth revolved around the sun?

Google

MUST TRY HARDER

What would be the consequence of having part of your large intestine removed?

A semi colon

Why is the circumference of a circle always larger than the diameter?

Too much pi

SCIENCE

Define the lunar cycle?

What astronauts use to get about on the moon.

What is the distinguishing feature of varicose veins?

They are very close together.

MUST TRY HARDER

Which part of the body secretes the hormone FSH?

The FSH tank

What causes dew to form on plant leaves?

The sun makes them sweaty

SCIENCE

Describe two reactions when you place a small piece of magnesium in a solution of sulphuric acid.

Surprise.

~~Amazement~~.

What name is given to an iron atom that's circular in shape?

a ferrous wheel

MUST TRY HARDER

What type of factor is involved in determining body mass?

How many doughnuts you ate

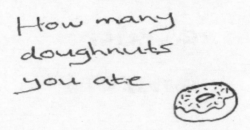

What is the common name for this compound: CH_2O?

SEAWATER

What are the main properties of zinc?

where you do the Washing up.

What is the definition of a planet?

A celestial body surrounded by lots of sky

MUST TRY HARDER

Name three food groups.

Fast. Frozen. Junk.

What is a phototropism a response to?

Pictures that make you look ugly.

SCIENCE

Give two properties that are the same for both radio waves and microwaves.

They both go up and down

Name two qualities that are unique to liquids.

You can drink them.
You can spill them.

MUST TRY HARDER

What creature is the natural predator of caterpillars?

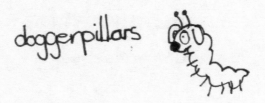

doggerpillars

What is the most likely reason why animals in hot climates have larger ears than similar animals in cold climates?

They don't need a scarf to keep them warm.

SCIENCE

According to Darwin's theory of
evolution, which males are most
likely to reproduce?

The ones with money
and a nice car

What happens to a boy's voice
during puberty?

He shouts at his parents

What is the significance of the Periodic Table?

It lets a woman know if she is pregnant

What is meant by the recreational use of drugs?

When people take them in the park

What does DNA stand for?

Definitely Not Able to answer this one

Name a major disease associated with smoking.

Death

What do you call the type of scientist who studies insects?

Mothematician

What is the function of haemoglobin?

He is a baddy in Spiderman films

SCIENCE

Define Boyle's Law.

After you switch the Kettle on, don't watch it.

What tests would you carry out in order to determine the sex of a chromosome?

Remove it's genes

MUST TRY HARDER

Why do we catch more colds in the winter?

Because germs hibernate in the summer.

What percentage of the population in the UK died from TB 100 years ago?

All of them.

SCIENCE

Describe photosynthesis?

A picture of someone
playing a keyboard

What turns red in the presence of an acid?

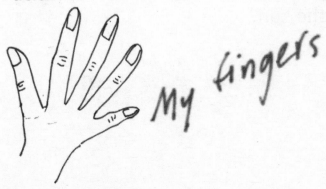

My fingers

MUST TRY HARDER

What does the red-shift from distant galaxies tell us about the start of the Universe?

Everything used to be more red.

What is the name for when the moon passes between the earth and the sun?

The end of the world

What is known as the 'building block of proteins?'

A mean old acid

Name a harmful micro-organism that could be killed by the use of antibiotics?

A Yorkshire Terrier.

MUST TRY HARDER

Name two alloys.

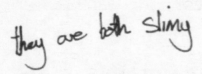

Iron Man and
The silver surfer

Name one way in which a slug and
snail are similar.

they are both slimy

Explain why using acids can be dangerous.

Bad trips

Look at graph 2. Harold did not use the deodorant on day 5 of the experiment. How can you tell this?

By how he smells

Otters mainly eat fish for food.
Which word describes their
feeding strategy?

Fishivore

Name a type of food that is a good
source of Vitamin A, C and D.

Alphabet Spaghetti

SCIENCE

In 2006, scientists agreed that
Pluto is not a planet. What were
their reasons.

*Because he is
Mickey Mouse's dog*

How are whales able to hear each
other's calls over long distances?

They use herring aids

The Hubble telescope is a satellite used for astronomical observation. Give one other use of satellites.

DEATH RAYS

In the image, why does magnet A repel magnet B?

Because it is so pugly

SCIENCE

Give an example of a food chain.

Aldi

What is one consequence of an increasing human population?

It's harder to get a seat on the bus.

MUST TRY HARDER

What phenomenon does the term
'hard water area' refer to?

The ice compartment
in the fridge.

List three ways that animals interact
with each other.

1. Kill each other
2. Eat each other
3. Do each other

Who explained that space and time are not fixed qualities and that both can undergo radical changes?

Dr Who

What two forms of energy are produced when something burns?

Running and screaming

When is precipitation likely to occur?

Just before cipitation

In the life cycle of a fly, what does a maggot turn into?

A PUPIL

Where would you find an artery?

In a gallery

What is the scientific name given to a material that does not allow heat to pass through it quickly?

A tea cosy

Robert has a frozen ice lolly. What can he do to stop the ice lolly from melting for as long as he can.

Eat it faster

What is the chemical formula for salt?

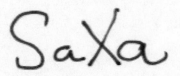

SaXa

SCIENCE

Where is the asteroid belt?

Just above the asteroid trousers.

Name three planets in the solar system.

Mars, the Sun, Vulcan

What name is given to the force that tries to pull a spacecraft back to Earth?

A gravity beam

Explain, in terms of electron configuration, why atoms of the radioisotope produced by the sixth decay in the U-238 disintegration series do not readily react to form compounds.

Because God made them that way

To change millilitres to litres you:

cross out milli

Give an example of a
'hermaphrodite'?

Marilyn Manson

Thomas's prediction about the experimental results was wrong. Give one reason why.

Because he is a stupid boy

What does the reaction between an organic acid and an alcohol produce?

A drunk organic acid?

SCIENCE

Which gas comprises 21% of
the atmosphere?

Air ♥

Whereabouts in the body would you
find the windpipe?

The rectum

MUST TRY HARDER

What is the main difference between an invertebrate and vertebrate?

Invertebrates are shy and prefer to stay at home

Name two examples of carbohydrates.

Chocolate Doughnut.
Jam Doughnut.

Which system in a female provides a place for a baby to grow?

Social Services

How would you set up a microscope and slide so the slide is ready to be viewed through the eyepiece?

I would put the slide in front of the eyepiece.

What substance is stored under the skin for insulation and to provide energy for release later when high energy food is in short supply?

A MARS BAR

Explain how plants reproduce.

Bees have sex with them

Why do plants grow towards
the light?

↑ Because its upwards ↑

What is the word equation for
aerobic respiration?

Breathe in. Breathe out.

Explain how dietary fibre helps digestion.

you could make a dining table out of it

Which part of a plant is responsible for seed development and reproduction?

The testicles

Give a possible evolutionary explanation for the shape of an egg.

So they fit into egg boxes

In computing, what is Mb an abbreviation for?

Mega bass

What are the young of frogs called?

Baby frogs

When you comb your hair with a plastic comb your hair will stand on end. What is the name for this effect?

Hair gel.

What is the main purpose of the skeleton?

Scaring people

What is Cu?

What you write at the
end of a text

What is it called when a solid changes into a liquid?

Magic

What is the first stage in the life cycle of a flowering plant called?

The garden centre

SCIENCE

Give an example of a noble gas?

Sir Hydrogen

Applying heat to a substance will cause its molecules to do what?

Warm up a bit

Which is the first part of the digestive system to come in contact with food?

The anus

Explain why you would weigh more on Earth than on the Moon?

There's more places to eat on Earth

SCIENCE

A high efficiency light bulb uses much less power than a conventional bulb. Explain why this is.

It doesn't come on for half an hour.

What name is given to the collection of 22 bones in the head?

A fractured skull

Why do people who work with radioactive samples take care to minimise their exposure to the radiation?

To stop them turning into super heroes

What does a mycologist study?

people called Michael

Millions of years ago, dolphins were dog-like creatures that lived on land. What made them leave the land to live in the sea?

Dolphins are rubbish at herding sheep.

What is another name for a Near Earth Object?

Armageddon.

If you fry an egg it is an example of a chemical change. Describe one visible change you could observe when an egg is fried.

In our house it disappears

Janice bakes a potato in her microwave oven then wraps the potato in aluminium foil when she takes it out. Suggest a reason why she does this.

Janice is going on a picnic.

An earthquake produces shock
waves in the Earth's crust.
Describe one effect of shock
waves on the Earth.

Panic.

Explain why planting more trees
may help reduce global warming.

Trees are cool

What do we call an animal that hunts other animals for food?

HUNGRY

What do we call an animal that is hunted as food?

Lunch

Nuclear radiation can be useful. How can nuclear radiation be useful to people?

Road safety. You will grow in the dark.

Give the name of one hormone that is usually in female contraceptive pills.

Easter Gem

Nuclear radiation is always present in the environment. What do we call this nuclear radiation?

Scary.

Colin's body mass is 100 kg and his height is 1.7 metres. Use this formula to work out if Colin is obese.
BMI = mass in kg / (height in m)²
BMI = ... 34·6
Is Colin obese? .... Yes
Explanation .... Pizza

The gap between the inner and outer brick walls of a house (the cavity) can be filled with:

Mice and spiders

New medical treatments are tested on animals before they are given to humans. Suggest why.

Rabbits won't tell anyone if it all goes wrong.

In the formula $E=MC^2$, what does C stand for?

Custard.

Give three reasons why the dodo became extinct.

It couldn't fly, it couldn't run fast and it was very tasty

What are the two main forces acting on a parachutist as he descends?

Screaming and sobbing

A car rolls to a halt with the engine stopped. Describe one area where a force of friction is at work.

Between the wife and the husband because he forgot to fill it up again.

Which class would an organism belong to if it has lungs, uses internal fertilisation and gives birth to live young?

An orgasm with lungs is classed as a mormon

The eye and the ear are examples of sense organs. What is the appendix?

A nonsense organ

Give an example of a reflex action.

swearing

What sort of organisms can be genetically engineered?

Crops, sheep, daleks

What is silicon dioxide (SiO2), the
most common constituent of sand,
used to make?

Egg-timers

What can cause genetic mutation?

Damaged jeans due to global
warming of the DNA in the
chrome ozone layer.

Give one reason why evolution led to beaks developing on birds.

Because beaks would look stupid on polar bears

Amplitude is the distance between the crest of a wave and the trough. What is the distance between the crest of one wave and the crest of the next wave called?

Surfing

According to the latest scientific observations, how old is the universe?

Very

What is Heisenberg's Uncertainty Principle?

I'm not sure

SCIENCE

Name two external forces that can exert change on an object's mass.

Eating. Dieting.

What is a Protein?

A tein that gets paid

Why does it take longer to boil an egg at the top of a mountain than it does at sea level?

Because you have to climb up the mountain first

What do you call the process in which electrons hook up in pairs?

Dating

SCIENCE

What is the primary difference between ethanol and alcohol?

People who drink too much ethanol dont need to go to a self-help group

What do you understand by the term 'resistance'?

You want me to take this stupid exam and I don't want to.

MUST TRY HARDER

What is a catalyst?

A reminder that you need to buy more cat food and litter.

Give a reason why there are over thirty different species of fruit fly.

There are over 30 different types of fruit

What was Sir Isaac Newton's most important observation about gravity?

Without it you can fly

What is a polymer?

Lots of mers

MUST TRY HARDER

What do you understand by the term 'quantum mechanics?'

People who fix quantums that have broken down

Name one of the fundamental rules of laboratory safety during a chemical experiment.

Never lick the spatula

What term is given to a group of stars that form an imaginary picture or shape in the night sky?

A constipation

Name three non-metal elements.

Earth, Wind and Fire

What is the common name for the collection of six bones commonly known as the 'hip bone'?

The Elvis

Name one characteristic of an amphibian.

It tells lies

What, according to Charles Darwin, is the most important factor for evolution to occur?

The organ of the species

What is an antibody?

The part below the antihead

MUST TRY HARDER

Where would you find a genome embedded?

In the garden with a tiny fishing rod.

According to popular legend what important discovery did Archimedes make when he got into his bath?

He'd put too much water in

SCIENCE

What was the main diet of the Brontosaurus?

Primordial soup

What is Artificial Intelligence?

CHEATING IN AN EXAM

A car reaches 120 mph on a straight road and has plenty of power left but can go no faster. Describe one of the forces that is stopping it.

The police force